MW01107112

EXPLORE CUBA
12 KEY FACTS

by Peggy Snow

12 STORY LIBRARY

www.12StoryLibrary.com

Copyright © 2019 by 12-Story Library, Mankato, MN 56003. All rights reserved. No part
of this book may be reproduced or utilized in any form or by any means without written
permission from the publisher.

12-Story Library is an imprint of Bookstaves.

Photographs ©: julianpetersphotography/iStockphoto, cover, 1; Kamira/Shutterstock.com, 4;
Zaneta Cichawa/Shutterstock.com, 5; James Bloor Griffiths/Shutterstock.com, 6; Rostislav
Ageev/Shutterstock.com, 7; Aleksandar Todorovic/Shutterstock.com, 8; Presidencia de la
República Mexicana/CC2.0, 10; baldovina/Shutterstock.com, 11; danm12/Shutterstock.
com, 12; possohh/Shutterstock.com, 13; akturer/Shutterstock.com, 14; user:akasenn/PD,
15; ADALBERTO ROQUE/AFP/Getty Images, 16, 17; Matyas Rehak/Shutterstock.com, 18;
Linda Hughes Photography/Shutterstock.com, 19; Lesinka372/Shutterstock.com, 20; Milosz
Maslanka/Shutterstock.com, 21; EvijaF/Shutterstock.com, 22; akturer/Shutterstock.com,
22; Lisa F. Young/Shutterstock.com, 23; Charlotte Arnold/Shutterstock.com, 24; Stefanie
Metzger/Shutterstock.com, 25; photosounds/Shutterstock.com, 26; Avaniks/Shutterstock.
com, 27; N. Vector Design/Shutterstock.com, 28; Nannucci/iStockphoto, 29

ISBN
978-1-63235-554-6 (hardcover)
978-1-63235-611-6 (paperback)
978-1-63235-671-0 (ebook)

Library of Congress Control Number: 2018940811

Printed in the United States of America
Mankato, MN
June, 2018

About the Cover
A city street in central Havana, Cuba.

Access free, up-to-date content on this
topic plus a full digital version of this book.
Scan the QR code on page 31 or use your
school's login at 12StoryLibrary.com.

Table of Contents

Cuba Is an Island Country

Cuba is a nation of islands. Most Cubans live on the main island. Many smaller islands lie off the coast. Most of them are uninhabited. Cuba is the largest country in the Caribbean Sea. Its total area is 42,803 square miles (110,860 sq km).

Several mountain ranges are scattered across Cuba. Sierra Maestra, Sierra Cristal, and Escambray are a few of the largest. Forests of evergreens and ferns grow on mountain slopes. Pico Turquino is the tallest peak at 6,650 feet (1,999 m). Mountains and hills make up one-third of Cuba. Lowland plains cover the rest of the country.

Fresh water sources are limited in Cuba. The country does not have many lakes or rivers. Streams tend

The capital city of Havana is located on the northwest side of the island.

It's a two-day hike to reach the top of Pico Turquino, the tallest peak in Cuba.

to dry up in the summer. The country is surrounded by salt water. The Atlantic Ocean lies to the northeast. The Gulf of Mexico is to the west. The southern coast is on the Caribbean Sea.

Cuba has many sandy beaches. Palm trees dot the white-sand shores. Coral reefs are common. Reefs stretch for thousands of miles along the south shore.

THE CORAL REEFS OF CUBA

Cuba has some of the healthiest coral reef ecosystems on Earth. Pollution has harmed many reefs around the world. Cuba's are thriving. Fish and marine life flourish among the reefs. Scientists believe this is because Cuba has not developed its coastal areas. Also, the land has not been over-farmed.

48
Number of miles (77 km) to Haiti, the closest neighboring country.

- Cuba is made up of a group of islands.
- Mountains, forests, and lowlands are common landscapes.
- Three bodies of salt water surround Cuba.
- Coasts feature sandy beaches and coral reefs.

Many Animals Thrive in Cuba's Warm Climate

Cuba is in a tropical zone. But it experiences a subtropical climate. Trade winds come in from the ocean. So do sea breezes. The Gulf Stream currents warm the nearby waters. Most days are hot and sunny. The average temperature is between 68 and 95 degrees Fahrenheit (20–35°C).

Severe weather blows in from the surrounding waters. Hurricanes are the most destructive storms. They usually occur between June and November. Heavy rains and strong winds cause flooding and damage. Most of Cuba's rain falls during hurricane season. The average annual rainfall is 52 inches (1,320 mm).

Cuba has many native animals. The bee hummingbird is the smallest bird in the world. It lives only in the forests and valleys. The Cuban Hutia is another species

The bee hummingbird weighs less than a US penny.

To help control the invasive lionfish, Cuba holds an annual fishing tournament to reduce the populations.

of animal known only to that country. It is a large rodent that lives in the forests. The colorful Cuban trogon is the national bird. It is found all over the main island. Bats, mongoose, crocodiles, and snakes also make their homes in Cuba.

700

Approximate number of species of fish and crustaceans in Cuba's coral reefs.

- Cuba experiences a subtropical climate.
- Hurricanes typically strike between June and November.
- The bee hummingbird and the Cuban Hutia are found only in Cuba.
- Fish and other animals swim along the coasts.

The waters surrounding Cuba are home to many fish. A few species are the angelfish, barracuda, and snapper. Manatees, whales, dolphins, and sharks swim along the coasts.

The lionfish is a recent invader of the Caribbean Sea. It has poisonous prickly spines that fan out across its fins. This predator eats large numbers of small fish around coral reefs. It scares away larger species, including sharks.

Europeans Took Over an Island of Indigenous People

Christopher Columbus arrived in Cuba in 1492. He claimed the island for Spain. Spaniards took control of Cuba in 1511. They fought and killed the indigenous people. They also brought new diseases to the island. Many indigenous people died from disease.

The British briefly took over Havana in 1762. The city was returned to

Statue of Christopher Columbus in the city of Baracoa, said to be the landing site of his ships in 1492.

49
Number of years Fidel Castro ruled Cuba.

- Spain began its rule of Cuba in 1511.
- Dictators ruled Cuba in the early 1900s.
- Fidel Castro formed a communist government in 1959.
- Barack Obama worked to improve relations between the United States and Cuba.

Spain a year later. Sugar production boomed during the 1800s. Enslaved people from Africa were made to work the fields. The Spanish ruled Cuba until 1898. The United States then helped Cubans defeat the Spanish. Cuba became independent. Dictators ruled in the first part of the 1900s.

In 1959, the revolutionary Fidel Castro and his army overthrew the government. The United States broke off relations with Cuba. Castro formed a communist government. He found new allies in the Soviet Union (USSR). Relations between Cuba and the United States grew worse. In 1962, the United States and the USSR almost went to war over Cuba. Over the next several years, many Cubans fled to the United States. Travel between the two nations was not allowed.

In 2006, Fidel Castro turned power over to his brother, Raúl. In 2008, Raúl Castro became president of Cuba. In 2014, US President Barack Obama started to improve relations between the United States and Cuba.

TIMELINE

1492: Christopher Columbus arrives in Cuba.

1511: Spanish rule begins.

1762: The British invade Havana.

1902: Cuba becomes independent.

1959: Fidel Castro and his army take control.

1962: The US and the USSR almost go to war over Cuba.

2008: Raúl Castro becomes president.

2014–15: Barack Obama works to normalize relations with Cuba.

Cuba Is a Communist State

For six decades, Cuba was led by a single family, the Castros. Fidel Castro was followed by his brother, Raúl. Both men served as president and head of the Communist Party. In April 2018, Miguel Díaz-Canel became the president of Cuba. Castro stayed on as head of the Communist Party.

In Cuba, the Communist Party controls all parts of the government. It is the only political party allowed. The head of the Communist Party is more powerful than the president.

The 31-member Council of State makes laws. The nine-member Council of Ministers runs the country.

Cuba has a large National Assembly of People's Power. This group focuses on issues that affect the country. Some of these are the economy, public health, and transportation. The National Assembly approves laws made by the Council of State. The government approves candidates for the National Assembly. In elections, a candidate must get at least 50 percent of votes. A seat remains open if this isn't achieved.

Raúl Castro succeeded his brother Fidel Castro in February 2008.

Granma is the daily newspaper of the Cuban Communist Party.

600
Approximate number of members of the National Assembly.

- The head of the Communist Party is more powerful than the president.
- The Council of State makes laws and the Council of Ministers runs the country.
- The National Assembly approves laws made by the Council of State.
- The Communist Party is the only one allowed in Cuba.

COMMUNISM IN CUBA

The Communist Party controls almost all aspects of life in Cuba. That includes the media. The government has authority over the news. It decides what information people receive. Some Cubans try to see different news online. But less than 40 percent of people have access to the internet. Freedom of speech is limited. Cubans who speak against the Communist Party are often jailed.

The Island Has Many Natural Resources

Tobacco takes up to eight weeks to dry.

Cuba has many valuable natural minerals. The country is one of the top 10 producers of nickel and cobalt. Nickel is a mineral found in the earth. Cobalt is produced from nickel. Reserves of limestone, rock salt, and marble are also found on the island. Cuba drills for crude oil with offshore rigs. This crude oil is refined and used to generate power.

One-third of Cuba has soil suitable for growing crops. Sugar, rice, and fruits are grown. Tobacco, coffee, and cocoa beans are harvested. Top agricultural exports include sugar and tobacco.

Cuba has few farm animals. Some cows, pigs, and chickens are raised. But the climate is not always good for animals, especially cattle. Many

THINK ABOUT IT

Cuba drills for oil in its surrounding waters. This oil exploration occurs near the United States. Why might US residents be concerned about this?

24,093

Number of square miles (62,400 sq km) of land used for agriculture.

- Cuba is a top exporter of nickel and cobalt.
- Sugar, fruits, and coffee beans grow well in Cuba's climate and soil.
- Many species of fish thrive in waters surrounding Cuba.

cows die from disease. Those that live produce little milk.

Fish are plentiful in Cuba's coastal waters. Tuna, sea bass, and tilapia are just a few thriving species. However, the shrimp population is in decline. Cuba restricts how many fish and crustaceans can be caught. The goal is to help species sustain their populations.

Sugar cane takes 12 months to reach maturity before harvesting.

13

Free Education Is Offered for Life

Students wear standardized school uniforms. They vary by school level.

In Cuba, education is important. From preschool through university, education is free to all. Children in school receive a lot of support from adults. School councils include teachers, parents, social workers, and health specialists.

Skilled professionals assist families with student learning. Parents are taught to instruct their young children. In after-school programs, students learn about the arts and develop social skills.

Teachers in Cuba are well trained. They receive ongoing instruction and mentoring. This focus on good teaching has produced results. Cuban children achieve at higher levels than their peers in other Latin American countries.

Formal education starts around age six. Students must complete

4,000

Estimated number of university students in Cuba.

- Cubans place a high value on quality education.
- Schools offer academic, social, and health support.
- Children must attend school through ninth grade.
- Students are required to pass an entrance exam to attend a university.

CUBA'S HIGH LITERACY RATE

Nearly all people in Cuba can read and write. The nation has a literacy rate of 99.8 percent. That is among the 10 best in the world. Literacy has been a priority since 1961. A campaign to teach reading and writing began that year. Educators were sent around the country to teach others. About 707,000 Cubans became literate in the first year alone.

schooling until at least ninth grade. A pre-university program or vocational school is the next step for those who continue their education. Students who want to attend a university must pass an entrance exam.

The University of Havana ranks highest among Cuba's more than 60 universities.

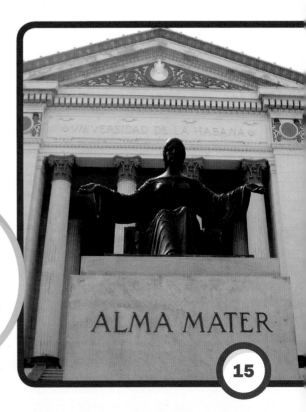

ALMA MATER

Cubans Do Important Scientific Research

The Cuban government values scientific discovery. It funds research in biotechnology, neuroscience, and other areas. These efforts have produced health care advances that benefit people around the world.

The Center for Genetic Engineering and Biotechnology (CIGB) in Havana employs 1,600 people. Labs here are spread out over more than 645,000 square feet (60,000 sq m). The Center of Molecular Immunology is also in Havana. Here Cubans have developed drugs and vaccines that are sold internationally.

People at the Cuban Neurosciences Center study the brain. Researchers map its activity to learn more about it. They also research age-related conditions. If screening can be improved, early detection might lead to better treatment outcomes.

Research takes place in the water as well as on land. Scientists in Cuba

Cuban scientists have made significant advances in vaccines for cancer.

The CIGB does research and development for more than 20 projects at a time.

study the coral reefs. This important work could help other nations replenish their reef ecosystems.

RESEARCHERS FACE CHALLENGES

Research in Cuba is often difficult. Internet service is limited. When it is available, low speeds can make it hard to send and receive data. Sometimes energy use is restricted. People can only use so much electricity. Scientific equipment often runs on electricity. Cuban researchers face another challenge. They can't buy scientific equipment from the United States because of the embargo.

9,350
Approximate number of researchers in Cuba.

- Cuba funds research in biotechnology, neuroscience, and other fields.
- Many Cubans are employed at research centers.
- Cubans have produced helpful drugs and vaccines.
- Researchers also study Cuba's coral reefs.

Cuba Is Trying to Modernize Its Infrastructure

Cuba's transportation and communication systems need updating. The country has asked other nations for help. Some companies are trying to start projects there. They want to help improve Cuba's infrastructure.

Getting around Cuba isn't easy. There is a railway system, but few routes that connect cities. Trains are slow.

Trains are maintained with secondhand and refurbished parts.

The system is run down. Equipment is in need of repair. But parts are hard to get. Fuel is scarce.

Main roads in Cuba are maintained. Rural roads are mostly in poor condition. They are often narrow and unpaved. Pedestrians and animals also use them. Few people drive cars in Cuba. Cars cost too much. The country is known for its use of old automobiles. Pictures show colorful American cars from

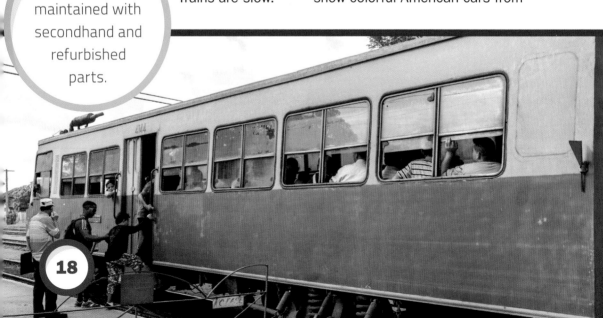

the 1950s. The government owns most of these vehicles. Until 2014, Cubans were not allowed to buy new imported vehicles.

Cuba's national airport in Havana offers domestic and international flights. Flights to other Caribbean islands are frequent. Cuba is working on renovating and expanding its airports.

About 12 out of every 100 people in Cuba have telephone lines. About 36 out of every 100 have cellphones. Service is expensive. The Cuban government has opened many Wi-Fi hotspots around the country. Those are expensive, too. Less than 40 percent of the population uses the internet. Private citizens are not allowed to buy computers. Email is limited.

Many cars in Cuba date from before 1959.

60,000
Number of cars in Cuba.

- Cuban infrastructure is outdated.
- The railway system is run down.
- Roads are often in poor shape.
- Telephone service is costly.

THINK ABOUT IT

Cuba's relationship with the United States has improved since 2014. More people are allowed to travel between the countries. Why might tourism be important to Cuba?

9

Cuba's Population Is Mixed

Most Cubans are paid low wages. But health care and education are free.

300,000
Approximate number of people who speak Haitian Creole.

- Most Cubans descend from Europeans.
- Spanish is the official national language of Cuba.
- Urban areas are the most heavily populated.
- The government promotes equality among citizens.

Most Cubans descend from Europeans. Spanish immigrants settled in Cuba starting in the 1700s. Other Europeans moved to the island later. Enslaved people from Africa were also brought to

Cuba. Some people started families with those of different ethnicities, including indigenous people. This has created some diversity in the population.

Havana is nicknamed the City of Columns for its architectural style that mimics ancient Greece and Rome.

children. Some worry they won't have enough money to raise them.

Spanish is the official language of Cuba. Many people use a variation known as Cuban Spanish. Other Cubans speak Haitian Creole. Immigrants from Haiti brought this dialect to the island.

Cuba is home to more than 11 million people. The population has increased during the past few decades. This is mostly because Cubans are living longer. The birth rate in Cuba has declined. Many people are choosing not to have

Most Cubans today live in urban areas. Nearly 80 percent of the people are in the cities. Havana is the capital and the largest city. More than 2 million people live there. Cubans in cities work mostly in service industries. People in rural areas often grow crops.

The communist government in Cuba tries to create a society of equals. It wants people to have the same social status. Most Cubans have similar possessions. Social relationships are more important than owning things.

10

Cubans Love Music, Dancing, and Celebrations

Live music is heard everywhere in Cuba. It seems that everyone in Cuba knows how to dance. Cuban music is a mix of African and European influences. Famous Cuban musical styles are son, salsa, bolero, and Latin jazz. Salsa is a very popular dance in Cuba. People also do the tango, the mambo, and the cha-cha-cha.

Other forms of art are important in Cuba. The island has about 250 museums. There are 2,000 libraries. Alejo Carpentier and Guillermo Cabrera Infante are two famous Cuban authors. Television shows and movies are limited. Still, going to the theater to watch a movie is popular.

Cubans enjoy celebrating holidays. January 1 is Triumph of the Revolution Day. This is the day when Fidel Castro first

Salsa is the most popular dance in Cuba.

came to power. May 1 is Labor Day. Cubans gather to hear patriotic speeches and watch parades. Cuba is famous for its cigars. Havana holds a cigar festival in February. Religious holidays were abolished in the 1960s. Pope John Paul II came to Cuba in 1998. During his visit, Castro made Christmas a holiday again. Raúl Castro made Good Friday a holiday in 2012, after a visit from Pope Benedict XVI.

People from Spain and Africa have had a lasting influence on Cuban food. Rice and black beans are eaten. Stews and meats are popular. So are pork sandwiches with cheese and pickles. This sandwich is called a Cubano. Plantains and other tropical fruits are lightly fried and eaten as snacks.

9
Number of national holidays.

- Live music and dancing are very popular in Cuba.
- Cuba has 2,000 libraries.
- Cubans celebrate the day Fidel Castro first came to power.
- People from Spain and Africa have influenced Cuban food.

THINK ABOUT IT

Every society has its own customs. What type of traditions does your country have? How were they formed? Research the origins of your cultural celebrations.

A traditional plate of roast pork, black beans and rice, and fried plantains.

Cuba Has Universal Health Care

Health care is free for all Cubans. This includes preventive care. People can have their blood pressure, heart rate, and other health indicators checked for free. Doctors and nurses live in the communities they serve. Doctors have between 1,000 and 1,500 patients. They must visit every patient at home at least once every year. Cubans needing other care are sent to clinics. Physicians in hospitals treat serious conditions and perform operations. Health institutes offer specialty care in different medical areas.

The government educates people on healthy lifestyles. It encourages people to eat well and exercise.

A typical family medical clinic in Havana.

Hospital Calixto García is a university teaching hospital in Havana.

Cubans learn about the health risks of smoking cigarettes and drinking alcohol.

Cuba spends less money on health care than wealthier nations. Prevention and early treatment help reduce costs. Cuba cannot afford most modern health equipment. The embargo with the United States limits access to many medical resources.

SO MANY DOCTORS

Cuba has approximately 90,000 doctors. There are eight doctors for every 1,000 people. That is more than places like the United States or the United Kingdom. Many other health professionals also provide care. Because there are so many doctors in Cuba, some travel to other countries to help people.

13
Number of medical schools in Cuba.

- Health care is free for all Cubans.
- Doctors and nurses make home visits in their communities.
- Clinics, hospitals, and health institutes provide additional care.
- Cuba spends less on health care than wealthier nations.

12

Daily Life in Cuba Has Challenges

Dominoes is played everywhere on the island, from big cities to remote rural areas.

Fidel Castro was in power in Cuba for almost 50 years. During that time, the nation's population underwent a big shift. People moved out of rural areas into cities. Some Cubans still work on farms, producing sugar or tobacco. But it is hard work. Most Cubans today live in cities. Large numbers work in hotels, restaurants,

$30
Average monthly salary in Cuba.

- Many Cubans live and work in cities.
- Independent businesses are new to Cuba.
- Shortages are common.
- Cubans enjoy music, dancing, sports, and games.

and stores. University-educated Cubans usually become doctors or engineers. Wages are low, even for highly skilled positions.

In 2010, 95 percent of all Cubans worked for the government. That year, Raúl Castro said more Cubans could become self-employed. They could open shops and cafés. They could drive taxis. They could hire their own workers. Cubans who wanted to be self-employed had to get a special license. In 2017, the communist government stopped giving new licenses for some types of self-employment.

The embargo with the United States started in 1960. It is still going on. It has led to many shortages over the years for the Cuban people. It can be difficult to get basic items like soap, toothpaste, and toilet paper. Food can be scarce.

Cuba produces electric energy from solar, wind, wood, and waste power. Water and electricity are often in short supply. People may go without them for hours or days. Buildings and homes are in need of repair. But people can't afford to fix them.

Despite many hardships, Cubans know how to have fun. People enjoy music and dancing. Many play sports. Baseball is the most popular sport. Soccer and boxing are favorites, too. Dominoes and chess are games enjoyed by many. People meet in parks to play them together.

A typical residential street in Holguín, a small city in eastern Cuba.

Cuba at a Glance

Population in 2018: 11,488,241

Area: 42,803 square miles (110,860 sq km)

Capital: Havana

Largest Cities: Havana, Santiago de Cuba, Camaguey, Holguin, Guantanamo

Flag:

National Language: Spanish

Currencies: Cuban Peso and Cuban Convertible Peso

What people who live in Cuba are called: Cubans

Where in the World?

Cuba

Glossary

barracuda
A large, aggressive fish in tropical and subtropical waters.

blood pressure
The pressure of blood as it moves inside blood vessels.

communism
A system where individual people do not own things like land, factories, farms, and mines. The government owns them, or the whole community.

coral reef
A collection of tiny animals that attach to each other and the ocean floor and capture food from the water.

crustacean
A sea animal that does not have a backbone but a shell or crust.

embargo
A government ban on imports and exports with another country.

indigenous
Native to a region or country.

mongoose
A rodent-like mammal with a long body and short legs.

normalize
To return to a friendly relationship after a disagreement.

revolution
An uprising to take over a government.

revolutionary
Someone who rebels against a government or ruler.

vaccine
A substance injected to prevent disease.

For More Information

Books

Paterson, Katherine. *My Brigadista Year.* Somerville, MA: Candlewick Press, 2017.

Murray, Julie. *Cuba.* Minneapolis, MN: ABDO Publishing Co., 2013.

Cavallo, Anna. *Cuba.* Minneapolis, MN: Lerner Publications, 2011.

Visit 12StoryLibrary.com

Scan the code or use your school's login at **12StoryLibrary.com** for recent updates about this topic and a full digital version of this book. Enjoy free access to:

- Digital ebook
- Breaking news updates
- Live content feeds
- Videos, interactive maps, and graphics
- Additional web resources

Note to educators: Visit 12StoryLibrary.com/register to sign up for free premium website access. Enjoy live content plus a full digital version of every 12-Story Library book you own for every student at your school.

Index

About the Author

Peggy Snow is the author of fiction and nonfiction children's books. She enjoys reading and researching all sorts of things. Minnesota is home to Peggy with her husband, child, and rescue dog.

READ MORE FROM 12-STORY LIBRARY

Every 12-Story Library Book is available in many fomats. For more information, visit 12StoryLibrary.com